Vintage Image

Birmir

GH01032689

by

Andrew Maxam

Andrew Maxam

**No. 2 in a series featuring postcards and photographs
from the twentieth century**

1. Six Ways, Erdington c1914, with the sign for the Queen's Head pub on the corner of Gravelly Hill North and Reservoir Road. In the background, Archer's Supply Stores was also a taxi service. That block was demolished after a traffic island was installed, over which the trams could proceed.

Erdington – A Brief History

In Anglo Saxon times, Erdington was a hamlet in the Kingdom of Mercia. In the Domesday Survey of 1086, it is mentioned as "Hardintone" and was held by Edwin of Mercia. Erdington's name has been spelt differently over the years; sometimes it's known as Yenton and even today, its inhabitants are referred to as Yentonians. Many of the familiar thoroughfares we know today were in place, such as Kingsbury Road and Chester Road which were part of an important network of routes essential for trade and survival to the village's Norman inhabitants. The powerful De Erdington family came to prominence around 1166 when Henry obtained the manorial rights from Gervais Pagenal of Dudley, thus beginning a long association between Erdington and the De Erdington family which lasted until 1467, when the family died out. Their tomb can still be seen today at Aston Parish Church.

During the subsequent years, the manor of Erdington changed hands many times; the Duke of Clarence and Sir Thomas Holte from the Holte family of Aston Hall being among the more notable landowners. Erdington Hall was built in the mid 1600s and was the manor house for Erdington until its demolition in 1912 to make way for the construction of the Tyburn Road. The prominent owners of the Hall included the Jennens family who lived there until the eighteenth century, Sir Lister Holte and William Wheelwright, who is believed to have given his name to Wheelwright Road. Erdington was very much a rural area until recent times. In the mid eighteenth century it had a population of fewer than 700 and consisted of 40 farms, 96 cottages, 2 smithies and a shop. The arrival of the canals at the end of that century encouraged some industrial development but the nineteenth century introduction of the railways was the spur to Erdington's suburban growth, seeing the population increase to 9,262 by 1891. One of the most remarkable events in the history of Erdington was the nineteenth century case of the murder of Mary Ashford by Abraham Thornton. The case made legal history because it was the last time that a man has been tried twice for the same crime in this country and the last time that election for trial by combat was allowed.

In 1894 Erdington separated from the parish of Aston, to which it had belonged since ancient times, and became a self governing Urban District Council with its own administrative centre at Rookery House (sometimes referred to as Erdington Council House), the former home of Dorothy Spooner, the wife of the anti-slavery campaigner William Wilberforce. The UDC was responsible for installing sewers and street lighting, building new houses, roads and footpaths. They were also responsible for building the Library, improving the transport system with the introduction of Erdington's first tramway and establishing three public parks. They also built Moor End Lane School so that children did not have to cross the busy High Street to get to Osborne Road School. In 1911, both Aston Manor and Erdington were absorbed into their expanding neighbour, Birmingham. It quickly became an important suburb of Birmingham, due in no small way to its good transport links: the Birmingham & Fazeley Canal, completed in 1783; the London & North Western railway line from Birmingham to Sutton Coldfield in 1862; the tramway in 1907 and its network of important roads. It has continued to evolve over the years. It was the first Birmingham suburb to be bombed in World War 2 when on 9 August 1940 a German plane dropped eight bombs in the area, resulting in the City's first fatality from Montague Road. The post-war era has been marked locally as in so many places by the sweeping away of many old, familiar landmarks. Shops, pubs, houses, cinemas, churches have disappeared, often replaced by buildings devoid of character. Wilmot House on Sutton Road was cleared to make way for the Lyndhurst Estate. Harlech Tower, built in 1960 was the first 16 storey block of flats in the city. In the 2000s the estate is again being redeveloped. No history of Erdington can be considered complete without mention of the infamous Spaghetti Junction or Gravelly Hill Interchange. Work started back in 1967 as part of a huge motorway link-up. It entailed diverting the course of the River Tame, demolishing homes and rehousing families. It formally opened in 1972. The village shopping centre declined in the 1970s partly due to lack of parking. The Erdington Town Centre Partnership has played a significant role in reversing this trend.

Stockland Green, to the south west of Erdington was primarily farmland (its name most likely is from the Old English word stoc, meaning an outlying farmstead). There were three farms locally which were swallowed up by council housing in the 1920s and 1930s. By the 1890s, terraced housing had appeared around Stockland Road. The built up area had increased by 1911 when the district came into Birmingham as part of Erdington and terraced housing lined much of Slade Road, much of it still intact today. The Bagot family built Pype Hayes Hall which lies in Pype Hayes Park. Close to the hall is Bowcroft Grove, recalling a field where two bowmen had their lodge. It was their duty to look after travellers who had to cross dangerous ground between Chester Road and Erdington. Pype Hayes takes its name from this house, not the moated Pype Hall. The word pype is thought to mean a pipe or conduit and to refer to a stream; Hayes means an enclosure within a chase or a manor. Again, after absorption into Birmingham, the area was fully built up and the Hall passed into the ownership of the city.

Andrew Maxam

Foreword

Andrew Maxam is one of a small group of people who not only are passionate about Birmingham's history but also are passionate about bringing that past to a wider audience. That deeply-held belief in sharing knowledge, photographs, postcards, memorabilia and whatever else is a vital one. Often we read of priceless works of art disappearing into the vaults of wealthy collectors who want only that they themselves can gaze at the beauty of what they have bought. In effect such a selfish action imprisons that artistic achievement, stifles it, and denies it the opportunity to reach out to peoples of different backgrounds and bring them together. Andrew is not such a person. For many years he has collected images of old Birmingham and for as long he has generously shared them with other researchers. Those images of Erdington can now be shared with an even wider audience, which through them can understand an integral yet independent urban village within Birmingham. I congratulate Andrew on his achievement.

Professor Carl Chinn MBE

Contents

Chapter 1 Gravelly Hill

2. The old Salford Bridge in 1924, two years before the new one was constructed. A tramcar no. 340 is on the 2 route, Steelhouse Lane to Erdington and a Midland Red Tilling Stevens single decker, no. OE 1137 is on the Birmingham to Streetly route.

3. A postcard view of Minstead Road, c1966. This popular residential area was a local community within itself although it suffered when many properties were demolished for the new Gravelly Hill Interchange (Spaghetti Junction) in the late 1960s and early 1970s.

Erdington Arms, Gravelly Hill

4. This view shows the Erdington Arms pub (nicknamed the Muckman) which stood on the Gravelly Hill / Slade Road junction, c1966. Now replaced by the Armada, the area is dominated by Spaghetti Junction.

5. Slade Road, (formerly Slade Lane) with George Road off to the right c1918.To the right of the tram stood the Star Picture Palace which closed in 1958. The row of houses next to the Palace was demolished for the Brookvale pub in 1934. Shops on the right included Mason's greengrocer; Hampton's butcher; MacDonald's stationers with the board advertising *Country Life* then the North Warwicks Laundry office. These shops are remarkably still intact today.

6. Slade Road, looking towards Erdington, with Hunton Hill off to the right, and St. Thomas' Road, left (see photograph no. 27) c1912. Ada Fanthom's stationer's shop was at no. 285 Slade Road on the corner of Hunton Hill. This scene is little changed today.

7. Slade Road, looking towards the city, this time with Hunton Hill on the left, c1918. The corner shop featured called "The Slade" was a tobacconists that belonged to Edith Adams who also published this postcard. Again, this scene is little changed today.

8. Not a motor car in sight as children gather in Hermitage Road which connects Clarence Road and Ashley Road, c1910. Note the incorrect spelling of Hermitage Road on the postcard caption.

9. A narrow boat on the Birmingham & Fazeley canal, outside the premises of James Collins, a hinge-maker and brassfounder, whose premises fronted onto Leamington Road, c1966.

Chapter 2 Pype Hayes, Tyburn & Bromford area

313/2   BURCOTE ROAD, PYPE HAYES ESTATE

10. Burcote Road connects Kingsbury Road and Tyburn Road. The Pype Hayes council estate was built in the 1920s on land which was predominantly rural in nature. This postcard was issued by William Shorrock, c1929, who ran the Post Office at 622 Kingsbury Road, near the Norton pub.

TERRYS LANE TYBURN

11. A man tends to his horse outside one of the many thatched cottages that used to stand in Terrys Lane (now renamed Eachelhurst Road) c1912. The rural nature of this area is well depicted in this scene.

12. The Wesleyan Chapel and Post Office stood at the junction of Kingsbury Road and Chester Road, c1910. Fine old enamel signs adorn the walls of the Post Office, including an advertisement for Sames Pianos of Corporation Street, Colman's Starch and Mustard.

13. Tyburn Road, looking out of town, with Inland Road on the left, and the former Bus Repair Works just out of view on the right, 1964. The lady is no doubt waiting patiently for the 66 bus up to Chester Road.

14. The junction of Tyburn Road with Kingsbury Road, 1933, after the installation of a traffic island that the trams could pass over. Just out of sight on the right, stood the now demolished Norton pub which was built in 1927.

15. Shops on Tyburn Road in 1963, looking out of town, just past Ansell Road, included Harrison's Hardware shop and a Cycle Shop which also sold Cleveland petrol and gave Green Shield stamps.

16. The Lad in the Lane (or the Ye Old Green Man), Bromford Lane, has been proved to be Birmingham's oldest pub building, with some timbers dating back to 1400. It has been a pub since around 1780. Here it is seen after a renovation when an Ansells pub in the 1930s.

17. Branch no. 46 of the Birmingham Co-operative, at 230-236 Wheelwright Road in 1963. Bromford Post Office is on one side together with Linthorn's Chemists; Smelt's tobacconists and Franklin's meats on the other side.

Chapter 3 Stockland Green

18. Edgware Road, when newly built, in the 1920s, looking towards Marsh Lane, with Barnet Road off to the right. A scene little-changed view today albeit with many more cars around.

19. Victorian houses in King's Road, looking up to Slade Road, c1912. The two waggons on view are advertising Hovis bread and McVitie's biscuits.

20. Stockland Green bus terminus, showing an early Daimler single deck bus on the 11 route, extended to Stockland Green in 1923. Behind the bus is Wilkins's chemists on the corner of no. 523 Slade Road.

21. Car no. 327 displays destination "Stockland Green to Steelhouse Lane" (allocated route no. 1 in 1915) at the original Stockland Green tram terminus c1912. Reservoir Road is off to the right. The route was later extended up Streetly Road in 1926 to serve the newly built council estate at Short Heath.

Chapter 4 Around Erdington Village

22. Shops on Boldmere Road c1919 included Aaron's Tea Stores, Parrott's Boldmere Paint Shop, Eastman's butchers and Bird's bakers.

23. A peaceful scene on Chester Road at the junction with Sutton Road, looking out of Erdington c1906. Today sees the road considerably widened and very busy.

24. A peaceful Gravelly Lane, looking from the junction with Station Road, with a row of shops including the Post Office, c1910.

25. A superb row of shops at Mason Road c1925 included Clayton's boot repairers; Dudley's confectioners (who published this postcard) and Mayhew's hardware shop at no. 61. Mason Road takes its name from one of Erdington's greatest residents, Josiah Mason who in 1869 built the landmark orphanage and almshouses at the junction of Chester Road and Bell Lane (renamed Orphanage Road). It survived until demolition in 1964. The Mason Road shops are still there today.

26. Penns Lane, at the junction with Beech Hill Road and Orphanage Road, looking towards Walmley, c1914.Trees have now grown up surrounding these old houses. This lane was the site of the murder in 1817 of a young woman, Mary Ashford, aged 20. The murder case went on to change English legal history.

27. A few locals gather for a chat in St. Thomas' Road, looking uphill from Slade Road to Rosary Road, c1920.

28. South Road, looking from the junction with Reservoir Road, with Ilsley Road off to the left, c1914. Some of these shops have now reverted to private houses.

29. Station Road (formerly Sheep Lane) looking towards the railway bridge and High Street, with Johnson Road off to the left, c1914. Erdington Railway Station opened in 1862 when the London & North Western Railway extended its line between Birmingham and Aston to Sutton Coldfield.

Sutton Road, Erdington, Bhm. 23.

30. A late 1950s view of Birmingham Road looking towards Sutton Coldfield, with Florence Road off to the left and Holifast Road on the right.

31. An empty-looking Watt Road, connecting Milverton Road to South Road, c1920.

Chapter 5 Erdington High Street & Six Ways

32. The upper end of High Street, with the Cross Keys pub just visible, left, on the junction with Station Road, c1932.

33. A similar view as above which shows a row of shops in High Street, at the junction with Edwards Road. Trams passed down Erdington High Street until the opening of the Sutton New Road bypass in 1938.

34. Road works in the High Street, c1938. A pleasant view of The Green and the High Street, probably photographed from the upstairs of Darrall's butchers shop.

35. A view of The Green, c1932, Darrall's butchers, centre and the library, left which opened in 1907. A Midland Red bus, registration no. HA2481, built in 1925, is bound for Streetly.

36. A view of The Green c1910, showing an open top tram no. 320 outside the Swan Inn. Note Shufflebotham's Stores on the corner of Wilton Road. The Green's ornate cast iron railings, lamp post and holly bushes have long since gone.

37. Shops on High Street with The Green, c1914. On the corner of Wilton Road at no. 59 High Street was John Wilton's butchers. Next door was Madame Leah Taylor's milliner's shop; Thomas Price's hairdressers; Whitehouse drapers, then the Post Office. These shops were demolished in the 1930s.

38. An early view of the High Street looking up to The Green, from around 1900, in the days when the clatter of horses' hooves echoed in the High Street.

39. Erdington High Street c1920, with the Palace Cinema, centre right, with the large notice board above the door. The cinema had opened in 1912 and closed in the 1970s to make way for a supermarket. Note the horse drawn milk float, left.

40. This 1955 view reveals that the Picture Palace, far left, was showing *The Long Gray Line* starring Tyrone Power, Maureen O'Hara and Robert Francis. Over the road, well known Birmingham shops such as George Mason and Midland Educational are on view.

41. A view of the High Street c1920, showing the tower of St. Barnabas Church, centre. Note the cart laden with twigs and branches.

42. The High Street, c1915 with Coton Lane on the left, looking towards the Church which is shrouded by tall trees. Next door stands the Acorn Hotel.

43. The same view some 40 years later in 1955 looking towards the Church, with Coton Lane on the left. Note the tramlines had been covered over by this time.

44. High Street, with Newman Road on the right and the Methodist Chapel, far right. The prominent sign on the roof gable was H W B Henn's furnishing store. Hughes's oil merchant was on the left hand side at the junction with Coton Lane, c1925.

45. High Street ,c1911, as seen from Six Ways with tramcar no. 103 heading for Birmingham. The Baptist Chapel, right, at the junction with Wood End Road was demolished in 1961 and rebuilt nearby. Next door to the Chapel is a sign for Elliott's furniture removers.

46. The Six Ways traffic Island c1955. Payne's shop was built on the site of Archer's supply stores. The three churches visible on this scene are St. Barnabas; the Methodist Chapel and the Baptist Church. Abbey Garage is prominent, next to the Baptist Church.

47. Six Ways looking towards the newly completed Sutton New Road and High Street in September 1938.

Chapter 6 Erdington Public Houses

48. The Bagot Arms, on the corner of Chester Road and Eachelhurst Road in 1962. The pub dates from 1931. The pub's name commemorates the Bagot family, occupiers of Pype Hayes Hall.

49. The Bromford in Bromford Lane on the corner of Farnhurst Road, as seen in 1962. It closed in 2008, to be replaced by housing.

50. The Leopard on Jerry's Lane, at the junction with Flackwell Road in 1962. It opened in 1940 to serve the Short Heath estate.

51. The spartan interior of the bar of The Leopard when new in 1940. Note the ornate cash register.

52. The Digby, Chester Road, Pype Hayes c1962. Formerly a social club, it is set quite a distance back from the road.

53. The New Inns on Summer Road in 1962. Formerly a Holder's pub before being taken over by Mitchells and Butlers. Still retains some beautiful etched windows.

54. The Norton, Kingsbury Road at the junction with Tyburn Road, c1948. Built in 1927, it was to close in 2000 and was later demolished. The site is now occupied by a supermarket.

55. The Cross Keys, High Street at the junction with Station Road, 1961. Built in 1911, replacing an 18th century inn, it contains some attractive Mitchells and Butlers stained glass.

56. The Rose & Crown on Gravelly Lane, c1962, in the days when it still had its "Vintner" outdoor. Its nickname is the Nose & Clown. Formerly owned by Butler's of Wolverhampton

57. The Royal Oak on Marsh Lane at the junction with Short Heath Road in 1959. It contains a very old window relating to Butler's Crown Brewery on Broad Street , in the days before William Butler joined forces with Mitchell.

58. The 18th century Swan on the High Street in 1962. The outdoor on the corner with Wilton Road was the former Shufflebotham's grocers shop. The Swan has now been rebuilt and is a much plainer building than before.

59. The Yenton, centre, seen here in the 1930s, near the Sutton Road tram terminus. The pub had opened in 1928. In 2007 it became Mitchells and Butlers' 200th Sizzling Steak Co pub, following an extensive refurbishment.

Chapter 7 Erdington Institutions

60. The entrance to St. Barnabas Parish Church which was built in 1824, when it was administered from Aston parish. Sadly the church was burnt down in 2007.

61. The Toll House on Gravelly Hill, c1935. A Turnpike Act was passed in 1807 covering the road from Birmingham to Erdington.

62. After much work by Mr. Charles Smith (headmaster of Osborne Primary School) of the Erdington Urban District Council, Erdington's Library opened in on 2 July 1907, financed entirely by Andrew Carnegie, the millionaire philanthropist.

63. An aerial view showing the Cottage Homes, bounded in this view by the railway, lower edge and Fentham Road, left and Reservoir Road, far right. Mr. W.C.Adams of the Aston Board of Guardians was primarily responsible for them. They were built in 1898 by Lee & Son of Aston. In the background is Highcroft Hall Hospital. They are now Grade 2 listed buildings and since 1987 have been administered by the Mercian Housing Association.

64. One of the many activities organised for the children included the Erdington Cottage Homes Boys Brass Band seen here proudly posing for the camera, on a postcard from around 1930.The band used to play in many competitions. Every year when they went on holiday, the band would march the children up to Gravelly Hill Railway Station.

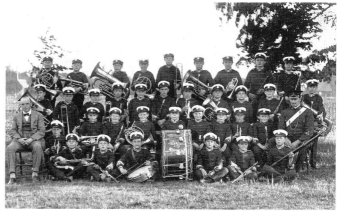

65. A procession on a summer's day in Station Road, taken from the railway station bridge, with Johnson Road, far right. This event was possibly a pilgrimage to St. Thomas & St. Edmund of Canterbury Roman Catholic Church, also known as Erdington Abbey, c1914.

Chapter 8 Erdington Leisure & Transport

66. Early motor cars parked in Spring Lane, c1931 on a winter's day. Note the front car has its radiator covered.

67. This horse and cart belonged to Mr Terry of Langley Heath Dairy and Farm, Erdington. The Terry's had a farm called Berwood on Chester Road for many years.

68. The first tram in Erdington, after initial opposition to the scheme, commenced 1 March 1907. Electric car no. 57 is seen at the Sutton Road terminus. Later extensions went to Short Heath (1926), Tyburn Road to Pype Hayes (1927).

69. Car no. 647 built in 1923-4 on the 2 route bound for town negotiates the Gravelly Hill junction on a damp September's day in 1937.

70. Open top car no. 233 built in 1907 is seen unloading at the Sutton Road terminus on a postcard dated 1909. The opposite shops had only recently been built. In Birmingham the terminus was at Steelhouse Lane.

71. The last day of the trams in Birmingham was on 4 July 1953. Tram no. 616 was 32 years old by the time it is seen here being cheered on by the crowds at Six Ways, opposite Chambers Garage in Gravelly Hill North. Those buildings on the right have recently been replaced by a Tesco supermarket.

72. Gravelly Hill Railway Station was opened in 1862 by the London & North Western Railway. This view looks towards Erdington, with Frederick Road running parallel to the railway line.

73. The bus here at Sutton Road terminus was bound for Sutton Parade. The registration no. of this single decker was O9942 and was built in 1923. Operated by Midland Red, double deckers were not allowed into Sutton until World War 2.

Brookvale Park 1909-2009

Brookvale Park was bought from the City of Birmingham Water Department by Erdington Urban District Council, and was the third to open after Rookery Park and Short Heath Park. The park's main feature is the former Lower Witton Reservoir, rendered redundant after the Elan Valley scheme came to Birmingham in 1904. See the back cover for a picture of when it was a reservoir. The park officially opened on 7 October 1909. Today the lake is an attractive feature with much wildlife in evidence.

74. The entrance to the park at the corner of Park Road and George Road c1910.The two small pagoda-style toilet blocks have survived; they are due to be refurbished as information posts. The bandstand hasn't fared so well, having been removed years ago. The bowling green is now bounded by a tall hedge. Note the spire of the chapel of Witton Cemetery visible in the background.

75. Another entrance to the park, c1910, taken from in front of what is today the Park office. The high ridge of Park Road can be seen in the background. The original railings have long since gone.

76. Children gather by the hedgerow next to the lake c1910. George Road runs off to the right. Today, many trees still overhang into the water just as they did a century ago.

77. Children dip their toes in the paddling pool on a summer's day, c1912. Note the rustic bridge leading to the water and the red brick built one crossing the pool in the background. Today, this area is overgrown and has returned to nature as a conservation area.